SilverTip

The House of Representatives

by Daniel R. Faust

Consultant: John Coleman
Professor of Political Science, University of Minnesota
Minneapolis, Minnesota

BEARPORT
PUBLISHING

Minneapolis, Minnesota

D1528877

Credits

Cover and Title Page, © Kamira/Shutterstock; 3, © Dan Thornberg/Shutterstock; 4–5, © Phynart Studio/iStock; 7, © Roman Rijkers/Shutterstock; 9, © Sipa USA/Alamy; 11, © SAUL LOEB/Getty; 13, © VP Photo Studio/Shutterstock; 15, © AFP/Getty; 17, © donald_gruener/iStock; 19T, © Vitalii Vodolazskyi/Shutterstock; 19B, © Win McNamee /Getty; 21, © stock_photo_world/Shutterstock; 23, © lev radin/Shutterstock; 25, © Sundry Photography/Shutterstock; 27, © sirtravelalot/Shutterstock; 28, © Kamira/Shutterstock.

President: Jen Jenson
Director of Product Development: Spencer Brinker
Senior Editor: Allison Juda
Associate Editor: Charly Haley
Senior Designer: Colin O'Dea

Library of Congress Cataloging-in-Publication Data

Names: Faust, Daniel R., author.
Title: The House of Representatives / By Daniel R. Faust.
Description: Minneapolis, Minnesota : Bearport Publishing Company, 2022. | Series: U.S. Government: need to know | Includes bibliographical references and index.
Identifiers: LCCN 2021030940 (print) | LCCN 2021030941 (ebook) | ISBN 9781636915999 (library binding) | ISBN 9781636916064 (paperback) | ISBN 9781636916132 (ebook)
Subjects: LCSH: United States. Congress. House—Juvenile literature.
Classification: LCC JK1319 .F38 2022 (print) | LCC JK1319 (ebook) | DDC 328.73/072—dc23
LC record available at https://lccn.loc.gov/2021030940
LC ebook record available at https://lccn.loc.gov/2021030941

For more information, write to Bearport Publishing, 5357 Penn Avenue South, Minneapolis, MN 55419. Printed in the United States of America.

Contents

From Roads to Reading

Where does money for roads, libraries, schools, and public spaces come from? The government pays for some of it! And who decides how the money is spent? In the United States, laws about how the government can spend money are made by the House of Representatives.

The U.S. government is divided into three branches, or parts. The House of Representatives is in the legislative branch. Together with the Senate, the House is part of a larger group known as Congress.

Libraries can get money from the laws made by the House of Representatives.

Representing the People

Congress is in charge of making laws. It is broken into two parts, called houses. The Senate is the smaller house. The House of Representatives is the larger. There are 435 voting members of the House of Representatives. The members speak for the state they are from.

The Senate has two members from each state. But in the House, the number of representatives for each state changes. It is based on the number of people who live there.

Congress meets in the U.S. Capitol building.

Becoming a Bill

How does Congress make laws? Every new law starts as a bill. One of the members of Congress writes the bill. Then, it goes to a **committee**. Committees are smaller groups of representatives. Each committee has a main focus. They may work on defense, education, or transportation.

Most laws can start in either part of Congress. But laws about raising and spending money for the **federal** government need to start in the House of Representatives.

Some bills set aside money to build roads and bridges.

#Infrastr

The members of the committee research the bill. They make changes until they agree on it. Then, the bill goes to the full House of Representatives. Members **debate** the bill and vote on it. If enough members agree, the bill is sent to the Senate for them to debate and vote.

Both houses of Congress must agree on the exact same bill. If even a word in a bill is changed by the Senate, the House of Representatives needs to say it's okay, too.

A busy day in the House of Representatives

House Parties

A lot of members in the House of Representatives vote the same way as others from their **political party**. Most representatives are in the Democratic Party or the Republican Party. These are the two biggest parties in the United States.

The party with the most members in the House is called the majority party. The party with the second most members is called the minority party. Sometimes, there are members who are from other political parties.

Political parties have different views on bills. But the best laws are made when representatives from all sides come together.

Speaking of the House

With all the different parties, bills, and committees, the House needs a leader. The Speaker of the House is in charge. They send bills to committees. They also give members their jobs in committees. When it is time to vote, the speaker counts the votes.

If the president and vice president were no longer able to do their jobs, the Speaker of the House would become the president.

Speaker of the House Nancy Pelosi *(right)* sometimes works with the president.

15

Checks and Balances

The legislative branch makes the laws. But the power of the House of Representatives has limits. No single part, or branch, of the government is too powerful. Each branch has powers to check, or limit, the power of other branches. They allow the branches to balance, or share, other powers.

The president can sign bills into law. Or they can **veto** bills that Congress has passed. This stops the laws.

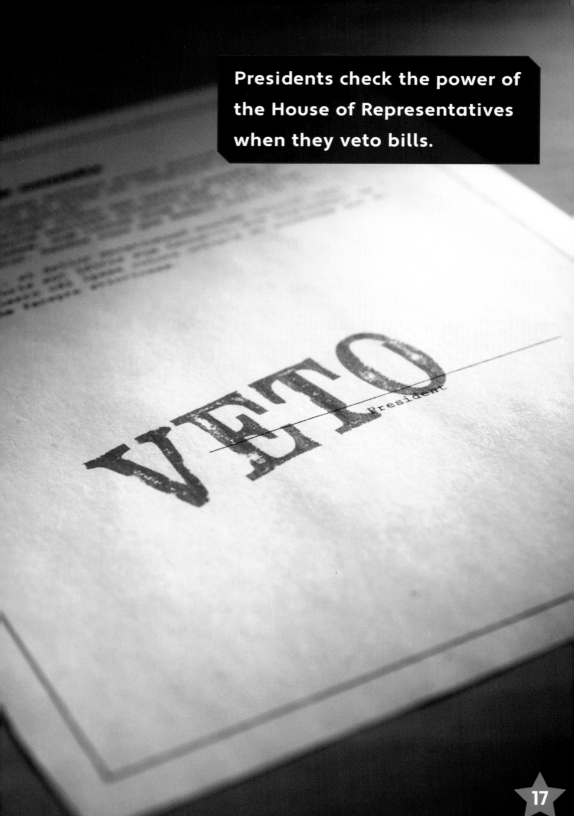

Presidents check the power of the House of Representatives when they veto bills.

The houses of the legislative branch share powers. Congress can check the **executive** branch. It has a say over how the president spends the government's money. The House of Representatives also has the power to **impeach**. This action can remove members of the executive and **judicial** branches from office.

Even the power to remove others from office has steps to balance power. The House votes to impeach a person. Then, the Senate has a trial. They decide if the person did something wrong.

Getting Elected

What does it take to become a member of the House of Representatives? Each member must be at least 25 years old to join the House. They have to be a U.S. citizen for at least 7 years. And they need to live in the state they want to represent.

Each member is voted into the House of Representatives for two years at a time. There is no limit to how many times someone can be a representative.

People do a lot to get the attention of voters during election time.

Do It for the District

Each member of the House is elected to speak for the people of a district, or area within a state. The United States is divided into 435 voting districts. Every state has at least one district. After that, districts are based on population. States with the most people have the most districts.

States are in charge of deciding where the districts are within their states. If they have more than one district, each district has to have the same number of people living in it.

Representatives listen to the people from their district to know what they want and need.

Every ten years, the government looks at where people are living. A **census** is a count of the population of the United States. The census helps decide how districts are broken up. States where the population grows a lot may get more districts. Places with less growth may get fewer.

The census used to be taken in person only. The 1960 census was the first one where people could respond by mail. In 2020, the census could be done online for the first time.

United States®
Census 2020

English
Go †

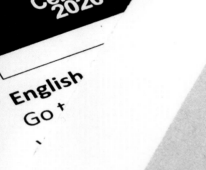

U.S. Census Bureau
Washington, DC 20233-0001
Office of the Director

United States®
Census 2020

U.S. Census Bureau
tional Processing Center
Logistics Avenue
ersonville IN 47144

CIAL BUSINESS

The Changing Face of the House

Districts may grow and shrink. And the lawmakers in the House of Representatives are always changing. Over the years, things in the House have started to look different. More women are being voted into office. The representatives are more diverse than ever. As the country changes, so do its representatives.

26

Congress makes laws for the entire country. That is why it is important for members of Congress to come from different backgrounds.

The Branches of Government

Legislative Branch	Executive Branch	Judicial Branch

Makes laws
Made up of the Senate and the House of Representatives

Carries out laws
Made up of the president, the vice president, and the president's cabinet

Says if laws are followed correctly
Made up of the Supreme Court and other federal courts

The House of Representatives

The House of Representatives is part of Congress. It has 435 voting members who work to make laws for the United States.

★ SilverTips for REVIEW

Review what you've learned. Use the text to help you.

Define key terms

bill   legislative branch
committee   representative
district

Check for understanding

What are the two houses in the legislative branch, and what are they called together?

Describe the steps needed for a bill to become a law.

Name one of the House of Representative's powers that is part of the checks and balances of government.

Think deeper

How does the House of Representatives have an impact on your life? Name at least one example.

★ SilverTips on TEST-TAKING

★ **Make a study plan.** Ask your teacher what the test is going to cover. Then, set aside time to study a little bit every day.

★ **Read all the questions carefully.** Be sure you know what is being asked.

★ **Skip any questions** you don't know how to answer right away. Mark them and come back later if you have time.

Glossary

census the official process of counting the number of people in a place

committee a group of people who are chosen to make decisions about something

debate a discussion between people who have different opinions about something

executive relating to the branch of a government that includes the president and vice president

federal having to do with the government of a nation

impeach to charge someone who holds public office with a crime

judicial related to the branch of government that includes courts and judges

legislative related to the branch of government with people who make laws

political party a group of people with similar values that joins together to impact the policies of government

representatives people who act or speak for a larger group

veto the power of a person to decide that something will not be approved

Read More

Connors, Kathleen. *How Does a Bill Become a Law? (A Look at Your Government).* New York: Gareth Stevens, 2018.

Kortuem, Amy. *The U.S. House of Representatives.* North Mankato, MN: Capstone Press, 2020.

McDaniel, Melissa. *The U.S. Congress (A True Book: Why It Matters).* New York: Children's Press, 2020.

Learn More Online

1. Go to **www.factsurfer.com** or scan the QR code below.

2. Enter "**The House of Representatives**" into the search box.

3. Click on the cover of this book to see a list of websites.

Index

About the Author

Daniel R. Faust is a freelance writer of fiction and nonfiction. He lives in Brooklyn, NY.